KIDS HAVE FEELINGS, TOO, SERIES

Sometimes I Feel Awful

By Joan Singleton Prestine
Illustrations by Virginia Kylberg

Fearon Teacher Aids

Editorial Director: Virginia L. Murphy

Editor: Lisa Schwimmer

Illustration: Virginia Kylberg

Design: Marek/Janci Design

Cover Illustration: Virginia Kylberg

Cover Design: Lucyna Green

Library of Congress Catalog Card Number: 93-72031

ISBN 0-86653-927-1
Printed in the United States of America
1.9 8 7 6 5 4 3 2 1

Sometimes my days start happy, then turn into jealous, impatient, selfish, mad, scary, sad, cranky, lonely, frustrating, ashamed, shy, left out, really tired days.

Today started happy. I had pancakes for breakfast, I got to wear my favorite shirt, and my friend David was coming over to play. Then things changed. Mom brushed Tricia's hair and told me to brush mine all by myself.

When Mom left the room, I messed Tricia's hair all up. Mom and Tricia didn't understand. I could have said, "Mom, I feel jealous. Brush my hair, too." But I didn't.

Then I waited and waited for David to come over to my house to play. When he finally got here, I was happy. I said, "David, let's go climb the tree." But David sat down and put together my house puzzle instead.

When he was finished, I said, "David, let's go climb the tree." David sat on the floor and put together my dog puzzle instead. One more time I said, "David, let's go climb the tree!" David ignored me. So I punched him. David didn't understand. I could have said, "I feel impatient. I waited and waited for you to climb the tree." But I didn't.

David picked up one of my games. I shouted, "That's mine! You can't play with it."

David didn't understand. I could have said, "I feel selfish. That's my game. I don't want to share it today. And besides, I still want to climb the tree." But I didn't.

9

Finally David was ready to go outside and climb the tree. I was happy. On the way out, he knocked over my block city. He tried to fix it. I yelled, "Get away from my blocks!"

David didn't understand. I could have said, "I feel really mad. I worked hard to build that city. Now it's ruined." But I didn't.

Finally David and I climbed the tree and
I was happy. We climbed higher and higher. The
branches started swaying and I started crying. David
didn't understand. I could have said, "I feel scared.
It's too high. Let's climb down." But I didn't.

When we climbed down from the tree, David said he didn't want to play with me anymore. He was going home, he said, because I was too cranky.

So David went home. Wheaton tried to make me feel better, but I shoved him away. I could have petted Wheaton and said, "I feel sad. David left. You're my only friend." But I didn't.

Instead, I kicked the dirt, stomped into the house, slammed the door, and shouted at Mom as she talked on the phone.

Mom didn't understand. I could have said, "I want to cuddle. I feel cranky about David going home." But I didn't.

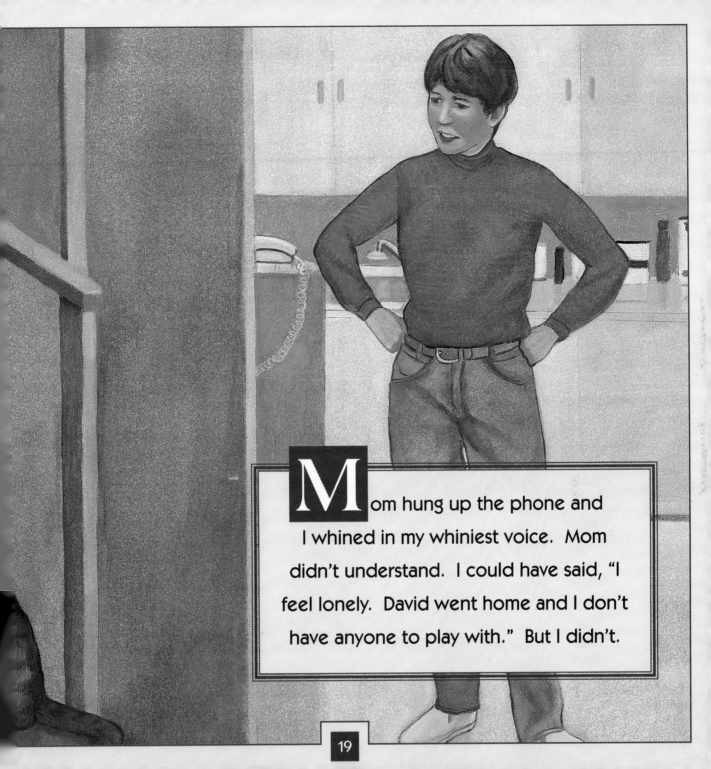

Mom hung up the phone and I whined in my whiniest voice. Mom didn't understand. I could have said, "I feel lonely. David went home and I don't have anyone to play with." But I didn't.

Mom wanted me to be happy. I wanted to be happy, too. But I was having a jealous, impatient, selfish, mad, scary, sad, cranky, really lonely day. And besides, no one understood how I felt.

Mom handed me a picture to color. I scribbled all over it. Mom didn't understand. I could have said, "Help me. I feel frustrated." But I didn't.

Mom took away the picture. She gave Wheaton a dog biscuit and me a cookie and a glass of milk.

Wheaton ate his biscuit. I ate the cookie and spilled my milk. I yelled at Wheaton and told him he was bad. Mom and Wheaton didn't understand. I could have said, "I feel ashamed. I'm sorry I made a mess." But I didn't.

The day got even worse when my brother came home from school. He brought home a new friend. I hid behind the chair and wouldn't talk. My brother and his friend didn't understand. I could have said, "I feel shy. I don't want to talk to someone I don't know." But I didn't.

After his friend left, Mom and my brother talked to each other in the kitchen. I jumped around, made strange noises and weird faces. Mom and my brother didn't understand. I could have said, "I feel left out. Please talk to me, too." But I didn't.

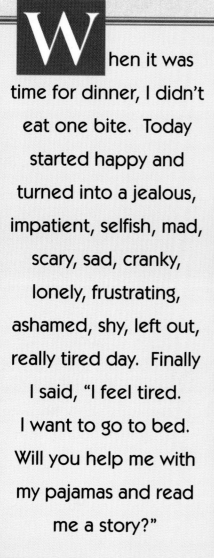

When it was time for dinner, I didn't eat one bite. Today started happy and turned into a jealous, impatient, selfish, mad, scary, sad, cranky, lonely, frustrating, ashamed, shy, left out, really tired day. Finally I said, "I feel tired. I want to go to bed. Will you help me with my pajamas and read me a story?"

"I have your favorite story right here," Mom said. "Come sit with me and Wheaton while we read and cuddle."

Finally Mom understood me. Tomorrow when I play with David, I'm going to tell him how I feel and what I want. Maybe tomorrow will be a happier day.

iscussing *Sometimes I Feel Awful* with Children

After reading the story, encourage discussion. Children learn from sharing their thoughts and feelings.

Discussion Questions for *Sometimes I Feel Awful*

- How was the little girl feeling at the beginning of the story?
- Did her feelings change? What happened?
- What feelings did she have in the story?
- How did she act?
- Did other people understand why she acted the way she did?
- Did they understand her feelings?
- What could the little girl have said in the story so others would have understood her feelings?

Significance of *Sometimes I Feel Awful* for Children

Sometimes a book will trigger strong feelings in young children, especially if they have experienced a similar situation. Encourage children to share their experiences, if they feel comfortable.

58,653

DATE DUE

E
Pre   **Prestine, Joan Singleton**
       Sometimes I feel awful

MEDIALOG INC
ALEXANDRIA KY 41001